NICK FLYNN

ALICE INVENTS A LITTLE GAME AND ALICE ALWAYS WINS

Nick Flynn's *Another Bullshit Night in Suck City* (2004) won the PEN/Martha Albrand Award for the Art of the Memoir and has been translated into thirteen languages. Flynn is also the author of two books of poetry, *Some Ether*, which won the PEN/Joyce Osterweil Award, and *Blind Huber*, which Stanley Kunitz called "an act of the poetic imagination unlike any other." He has been awarded fellowships from the Library of Congress, the Amy Lowell Trust, the Fine Arts Work Center, and the John Simon Guggenheim Foundation. Some of the venues his poems, essays, and nonfiction have appeared in are *The New Yorker*, the *Paris Review*, National Public Radio's *This American Life*, and *The New York Times Book Review*. He teaches one semester a year at the University of Houston and spends the rest of the year elsewhere.

ALSO BY NICK FLYNN

ALICE INVENTS A LITTLE GAME
AND ALICE ALWAYS WINS

ALICE
INVENTS A
LITTLE GAME
AND
ALICE
ALWAYS WINS

NICK FLYNN

FARRAR, STRAUS AND GIROUX

NEW YORK

Farrar, Strauss & Giroux
18 West 18th Street, New York 10011

Printed in the United States of America
First edition, 2008

Library of Congress Cataloging-in-Publication Data
Flynn, Nick, 1960–
    Alice invents a little game and Alice always wins / Nick Flynn.
    p.   cm.
    ISBN-13: 978-0-86547-985-2 (pbk. : alk. paper)
    ISBN-10: 0-86547-985-2 (pbk. : alk. paper)
    1. Friends—Drama.   2. New York (N.Y.)—Drama.   3. Electric power failures—
Drama. I. Title.

PS3556.L894A79 2008
812'.54—dc22

2007052772

Design and illustrations by Aaron Artessa

www.fsgbooks.com

P1

FOR LILI

ACKNOWLEDGMENTS

I owe huge debts of inspiration to the following:

Cornelius Eady, who opened a door by approaching me with the idea of writing a play.

Sarah Stern, who followed through with this idea.

Tehching "Sam" Hsieh, the Taiwanese-born artist who spent a year (1981 to 1982) living outside in New York City ("The Outdoor Piece").

Linda Montano, who spent a year (1983) tied by an eight-foot rope to Tehching Hsieh.

Deborah Ash (*mwalimu*) and Hubert Sauper (*rafiki*), who invited me to walk through Tanzania with them.

The amazing actors and directors of the staged readings, who offered invaluable insights.

Doug Montgomery, who shared his research into the syntax of the joke.

Esra Padgett, vernacular consultant and linguist extraordinaire.

Mel Chin, who urged me not to let people muscle me.

William Stafford, who pointed out that "the darkness around us is deep."

Mark Subias and Denise Oswald, who shepherded this book into existence.

ALICE INVENTS A LITTLE GAME
and ALICE ALWAYS WINS

PRODUCTION HISTORY

Alice Invents a Little Game and Alice Always Wins was commissioned
by Vineyard Theatre, New York City, with support from the National
Endowment for the Arts.

The play was workshopped as part of the Vineyard Theatre/Poetry
Theatre Project in November 2003, in New York City. Director: Ken
Rus Schmoll. Producer: Sarah Stern. Stage Manager: Michael McGoff.

ALICE *Deidre O'Connell*
GIDEON *Tim Hopper*
ESRA *Leo Kittay*
IVAN *Maria Dizzia*

An expanded version of *Alice* was workshopped by the Vineyard
Theatre in 2006. Director: Bob McGrath.

ALICE *Lili Taylor*
GIDEON *Mike Myers*
ESRA *Maria Dizzia*
IVAN *Tim Hopper*

Alice was presented as part of City University of New York's
Prelude Festival in 2006. Reading Director: Bob McGrath. Stage
Director: William Salicath.

ALICE *Elizabeth Marvel*
GIDEON *Patrick McNulty*
ESRA *Esra Padgett*
IVAN *Quentin Mare*

CHARACTERS

ALICE, female, thirty to fifty years old
GIDEON, male, mid-forties
ESRA, female, fifteen years old
IVAN, male, mid-thirties

SETTING

New York City

ACT ONE
SCENE 1

Stage dark. A television flickers on—a nature show: Africa, the Serengeti. Hyenas circle a dying gazelle. Lights up. Late afternoon. ALICE, *somewhere between thirty and fifty years old, sits erect in an armchair on a city sidewalk, her back against an electronics store window, reading a newspaper. She is dressed in layers but not shabby. Her demeanor is somewhat haughty, almost imperious—the chair is her throne. The television is in the window, behind and slightly above her head. As* ALICE *reads, the door to her right opens, and* GIDEON *steps out—mid-forties, suit jacket, jeans. He seems dazed, stares straight ahead. The door clicks shut behind him. He starts, pats his pocket for the key, turns and tries the door—door is locked. Checks his pockets for the key. No key. Pauses. Rubs temple. Puts hand on knob, gives it a good shake. Nothing. Tries harder, like opening a jar. Glances at* ALICE, *who is seemingly focused on reading her newspaper.* GIDEON *tries the knob delicately, like a safecracker. Nothing. Takes off his jacket, turns pockets inside out searching for key.* GIDEON *looks at* ALICE, ALICE *glances at him.* GIDEON *gestures that he's locked himself out.* ALICE *raises an eyebrow.*

GIDEON: I live here.

ALICE *shrugs.* GIDEON *puts his coat back on, the pockets hanging out.*
GIDEON *looks at the names on the bells. Looks at* ALICE.

GIDEON: My name isn't on the bell yet. (*Scans names.*) This one
should be me.

From her chair, ALICE *squints at bells, clucks her tongue, goes back to
her newspaper.* GIDEON *tries door again, subtly presses shoulder
against it.* ALICE *half watches over the top of newspaper, skeptical.*
GIDEON *takes doorknob in hand; kicks once, ineffectually, at bottom of
door.* GIDEON *leans away from door, then throws his shoulder against
it. Door doesn't budge.* ALICE *smiles, shakes head knowingly. Near
defeat,* GIDEON *leans head wearily against the door, stares down length
of the sidewalk, away from* ALICE. *As* ALICE *speaks,* GIDEON *turns
slowly to listen.*

ALICE (*reading from newspaper, to no one in particular*): The
question, turns out, is not why we sleep, but why we wake up.
(*Looks up matter-of-factly.*) Dreaming. (*To* GIDEON) Dreaming is
the more natural state—consciousness, this (*looks around*) . . . this
is unnatural.

GIDEON *stares at her, failing to understand the significance.* ALICE
folds newspaper, slowly stands, moves to GIDEON. *He stiffens.* ALICE
taps his chest with the newspaper.

ALICE: Scientifically there's no reason to wake up.

Using the folded newspaper, ALICE *moves* GIDEON *a few inches away from bells, then looks at the names on bells for a moment, her finger hovering over them. She presses one, waits, listens. Nothing.*

ALICE: No one home.

GIDEON: I live alone.

ALICE: Is that how it is? (*Walks back to chair.*) Nice to have the place to yourself. (*Sits, looks at* GIDEON *intently.*) You can walk around naked.

GIDEON*'s eyes widen.* ALICE *opens newspaper.* GIDEON *looks at bells.*

GIDEON: I'll ring my neighbor. We pass each other in the hall. We've never spoken . . .

ALICE: Neighbors can be good. But you should be careful.

GIDEON *looks at* ALICE. *Looks at bells. Rings a bell. Waits. He is about to ring again when intercom speaks, nearly unintelligible.*

INTERCOM: Whoizit?

GIDEON: Hi, uh. I live in the apartment beside you. I've locked myself out. Apartment thirteen.

INTERCOM: (*Unintelligible static.*)

Silence. GIDEON *hesitates, then rings again.*

GIDEON: Do you think you could buzz me in?

Silence. Reluctantly he rings the bell again. Intercom clearer now, annoyed.

INTERCOM: What?
GIDEON: Could you buzz me in? I've locked myself out. If I could use your phone . . .
INTERCOM (*nearly unintelligible*): Jesus H. Christ.

As intercom speaks, the door buzzes for a second. GIDEON, *surprised, lurches toward it, but too late.* GIDEON *glances at* ALICE. *Rubs temple. Looks at bells again. Straightens himself. Presses bell.*

GIDEON: Sorry. I missed it that time. (*Beat.*) I'm not feeling well. I wonder if you could buzz me in again?

Silence. ALICE *shakes head knowingly. On the television, a million wildebeests migrate northward.* ALICE *stands, moves beside* GIDEON.

ALICE: You gotta be careful with neighbors. They can turn on you. (ALICE *squares shoulders, rings bell, hisses softly into mouthpiece.*) You have to come out sometime, bitch.

GIDEON *looks aghast.* ALICE *sits back down, takes off her shoes, rubs feet.*

ALICE: I had a neighbor like that.

GIDEON *straightens his jacket collar.*

ALICE: Behind on the rent?

GIDEON *shakes head. Notices his pockets turned inside out, tucks them in.*

ALICE: That's how it starts—show up late a few times, get the sack, the money dries up . . .
GIDEON: Money is not a problem.

GIDEON *takes out wallet, pulls out a credit card, shows it to* ALICE. GIDEON *looks at door, looks at card, tries to jimmy door with card.*

GIDEON: Not a problem at all. (*Card snaps in half.*) Goddammit.
ALICE: That's a good lock on that door, as I recall. Does what you want a lock to do.

GIDEON *glares at her.*

ALICE: Beg, borrow, get someone else to pay, you have to keep up on the rent.
GIDEON: Listen, I'm not behind on the rent. I've locked myself out.
ALICE: I don't see you heading off to work every morning. Not lately.
GIDEON: That's . . . temporary. I'm between things. (*Flutters hand vaguely up at building.*) Working at home for now.
ALICE (*holds up newspaper*): Me too.

GIDEON *almost smiles.*

GIDEON: Do you know the landlord's name? The woman we're subletting from never told me.

ALICE: Oh, I wouldn't do that. Tell the landlord? What's to keep him from sliding someone else in?

GIDEON *considers this.* ALICE *pulls a cell phone from the chair cushions, holds it casually up to* GIDEON.

ALICE: Why don't you call a locksmith?

GIDEON *looks dubiously at the cell phone.*

ALICE (*looks more intently at* GIDEON): I found it in the park.

GIDEON *shakes his head slightly, turns away, leans his head against the door.*

Blackout.

SCENE 2

Lights up. Morning. Television off. GIDEON *is squeezed in beside* ALICE *on the chair, asleep with his head on her shoulder. His suit collar is turned up, his hair disheveled.* ALICE *is reading a book. As* ALICE *reads,* GIDEON *slowly wakes up, realizes he's been leaning on her. Embarrassed, he straightens himself but remains sitting beside her. A box of donuts is balanced on the arm of the chair beside* ALICE—*she takes one. She comes upon a passage in the book, eats donut as she speaks.*

ALICE (*musing*): Straw to a drowning man. *Straw* to a drowning man. A drowning man. A man drowning. (*Beat.*) I've never been able to wrap my mind around that one—You see a man drowning, you throw him a straw. (*Beat.*) What exactly does the drowning man do with the straw? I mean, does he use it like a snorkel, to breathe underwater? Does he simply hold on to it, like a tiny life raft—Hey, drowning guy, grab onto this, a thousand more and you got yourself a boat. Does he use it to drink the ocean or puddle or whatever it is he's drowning in, thus hurrying his demise, ending his misery? Is it the same straw that broke the camel's back, the proverbial "last straw," that last little bit which somehow pulls him under? (*Looks at* GIDEON.) What kind of straw are we talking about here?

GIDEON *looks at* ALICE. *He stands, looks around, still groggy. Phone rings.* GIDEON *looks around for source of sound.* ALICE *pulls cell phone from chair cushions, opens it.*

ALICE: Who? He's not here. What? *Your* phone? How do I know that? (*Closes phone, then speaks to audience.*) Straw. I mean, you're close enough to hand him a straw, or a piece of straw, why don't you take his hand and pull him out?
GIDEON: That phone works?
ALICE: I told you. (*Takes another donut from the box, offers it in an offhand way.*) You hungry?

GIDEON: No. Could I . . . ?

ALICE *passes* GIDEON *the phone. He turns it over suspiciously in his hand, opens it, dials 411, listens.*

GIDEON: It's got no credit.
ALICE (*dawns on her*): Incoming. Try collect.

GIDEON *closes phone, hands it back to* ALICE. ESRA, *a fifteen-year-old girl, rides up on a foot-propelled scooter. She parks it, goes to bells, rings one, waits. Looks up at building. Tries door. Turns to* ALICE.

ESRA: Power's out. School told us to go home. (*Beat.*) Have you seen my mom?
GIDEON: Power's out?
ESRA (*ignores* GIDEON—*to* ALICE, *with playful urgency*): This morning, in the playground, millions of business guys were sleeping beneath the jungle gyms. In suits! They looked laminated.
ALICE: Your mom's not back yet.
ESRA: Figures.
ALICE (*dawns on her*): The trains, listen—they're dead.

All cock their heads, listen.

ALICE: Why, when the power fails, do trains stop running? Since when do trains need light to move? I thought they made their own light.

GIDEON: You're the girl who lives next door. I don't suppose you could let me use your phone? I've locked myself out.

ESRA: Next door?

GIDEON: To me. I live in thirteen.

ESRA: Agnes lives in thirteen.

ALICE: He's behind on the rent.

GIDEON: I'm not behind on the rent. I'm . . . we're . . . subletting from Agnes.

ALICE: I thought you lost your job?

GIDEON (*to* ALICE): I've just locked myself out. (*To* ESRA) Look, I know you can't just let a strange man inside your building, but if your mother is home, could you ask her to buzz me in?

ALICE *and* ESRA *look at each other, laugh.*

ALICE: Her mother isn't home.

ESRA (*to* ALICE): If you see my mom, will you tell her I was here?

ALICE: Sure, sweetie. Take a donut.

ESRA *takes a donut, fetches scooter, rides off.* GIDEON *looks up at sky, hunches shoulders, turns up his jacket collar.*

GIDEON: Looks like rain. Looks like it's gonna pour. What do we do when it rains?

ALICE (*still watching* ESRA *ride away*): It'll pass right over us.

GIDEON *considers this, looks doubtfully at the sky; turns toward television, though it is dead.*

ALICE (*teasingly ominous*): Maybe soon it'll be your clothes, raining down. (*Puts hands playfully over her head.*) I better watch out. (*More seriously*) What'd she do, toss you out? (*Beat.*) Happened to me. My husband, we'd fight all the time—I couldn't promise I'd meet him in eternity. Eternity! Ha!

GIDEON *sighs heavily but doesn't respond. The television flickers on— Africa, tribal dancing.* GIDEON *stares at it. Looks down at* ALICE. *At donuts.* GIDEON *goes to bells. Rings them all. A voice comes over the intercom.*

INTERCOM: Yes?
GIDEON: Gas man.
INTERCOM: What?
GIDEON: Gas man. Here to check the meters.
INTERCOM: Jesus H. Christ.

The door buzzes, GIDEON *pulls it open; steps inside; looks down at* ALICE, *slightly pained; shrugs; lets it close behind him. Television flickers off.*

Blackout.

SCENE 3

Stage dark. Television flickers on—Africa. A lion watches the wildebeest migration. Lights up. Morning. GIDEON *is standing, facing window, watching television. The door is propped open with his jacket.* IVAN, *mid-thirties, is lying facedown on the sidewalk about five feet away, wearing an expensive suit.* ALICE *is nowhere to be seen. The box of donuts sits where* ALICE *had been sitting, the words DROWNING? FREE STRAWS written on the open lid.* IVAN *rouses himself and stands, stretching.* IVAN *sees* GIDEON, *sizes him up, walks over, stands close. Speaks while half watching television.*

IVAN: Wildebeests. (*Glances at* GIDEON—*no response.*) Three million stumbling north for the last mouthful of grass. The lions, they reach in, pluck 'em like daisies. Like after-dinner mints.

GIDEON *half glances at* IVAN, *then back to television.*

IVAN: Three years ago, I spent a week on safari. The Serengeti. Ngorongoro. A week under the stars with a .45 under my head. Hadn't slept outside since. Feels good. Alive.

No response from GIDEON. IVAN *leans in closer, lowers voice.*

IVAN: One morning, I'm pissing in a river—this crocodile, he's eating a zebra, not five feet from my boot. He's stripped the whole body clean, but the head, the head's giving him trouble.

GIDEON *half glances at* IVAN, *leans slightly away.*

IVAN: He keeps gnawing at it but he can't make any progress.

No response from GIDEON.

IVAN: The head was too big. (*Realizes television is on, points to it.*)
Hey, the power's back.

GIDEON: It's been flickering all night. Impossible to sleep.

IVAN: I can sleep through anything. What time is it?

GIDEON (*looks up at sky*): Almost seven, I'd guess.

IVAN: Trains running? You headed downtown?

GIDEON: No. I live here.

IVAN: Serious? (*Taps* GIDEON *on shoulder, points to door.*) Let me use
your bathroom. I gotta clean up.

GIDEON: I'm locked out.

IVAN (*indignant snort*): Come on.

GIDEON: No, really.

IVAN (*annoyed*): You got electric locks or something? (*Shakes head,
laughs.*) Shit, to be stuck outside your own fucken door all night. I
thought I had it bad. (*Beat. Holds out hand to* GIDEON.) Ivan.

GIDEON (*looks at hand, takes it briefly*): Gideon.

IVAN (*notices box of donuts, nods toward it*): Yours?

GIDEON *looks at donuts.* IVAN *takes a donut.*

IVAN: You mind?

IVAN *takes bite of donut. They look at television.*

IVAN: Fucken Africa. It's a cartoon world down there, everything the
wrong size—the leaves, the trees, the bugs. Bigger than life.

Everywhere you turn, you think, *That* could kill me, *that* could kill me. The water, a cut on your knee, a mosquito. The sun, my God, the sun. (*Points to* GIDEON's *face.*) It's the things you can't see that'll get you. (*Musing, takes bite of donut.*) I felt so hungry all the time, like *I* was the one starving. Nothing but rice and sauce, rice and sauce, Jesus Christ, I'd shovel it in. (*Takes bite of donut.*) Must have gained ten fucken pounds.

GIDEON *looks briefly up and down* IVAN's *body.*

GIDEON: You wouldn't have a phone I could use?
IVAN (*comes out of his reverie, looks at* GIDEON): A phone?
GIDEON: I need to call a locksmith.
IVAN: Maybe there's an open window out back. I could give you ten fingers.
GIDEON: An open window?
IVAN (*steps back, looks up at building*): Or if we could get onto the roof, I could tie a rope around you, lower you down.
GIDEON: You don't have a phone?
IVAN: Ran out of juice last night. (*Points to television.*) But the power's back.

IVAN *pushes last of donut into his mouth while looking at* GIDEON. *Wipes mouth with sleeve.*

IVAN: I have to get downtown. Gideon, it's been good talking to you. (*Sincerely*) It helps.
GIDEON (*confused*): Sure.

IVAN *offers* GIDEON *his fist for fist bumps.* GIDEON *tentatively fist-bumps.*

IVAN: Don't let them muscle you, brother.

IVAN *straightens his tie in the window, wanders off.* GIDEON *moves to* ALICE'*s chair, picks up box of donuts, sits, turns box over in his hands. A shirt flutters down on his head, followed by another, followed by a duffel bag, which thumps onto the ground beside him.*

Blackout.

ACT TWO
SCENE 1

Lights up. Morning. Television off. GIDEON *faces audience, standing in front of* ALICE's *chair.* GIDEON *is surveying his belongings, which are in piles on the sidewalk around him. The open box of donuts is still on chair.* ESRA *rides up on scooter, rings bell, stands back, looks up at windows.*

ESRA (*notices* GIDEON): Have you seen my mother?
GIDEON (*doesn't look at* ESRA, *self-absorbed*): Your mother? Not
    really.

ESRA *makes a disdainful face.* GIDEON *surveys his stuff, bends to look in a suitcase.* ESRA *looks down at his stuff, moves in closer, bends and picks a cassette tape from a box.*

ESRA: Is Pink Flag the band, or Wire?
GIDEON: Hmm?
ESRA: Pink Flag—how much?

GIDEON *stares at cassette, slowly reaches out and takes it from* ESRA's *hand.*

GIDEON: Oh, no. It's not . . . for sale. I'm just . . . organizing.

GIDEON *bends to replace cassette in box, drops to his hands and knees, continues ordering his piles of things.*

ESRA: Oh.
GIDEON (*distracted*): One accumulates an amazing amount, over time.

ESRA *sits on a box, picks up a guitar, strums it tentatively. At sound of guitar,* GIDEON *looks up from hands and knees, seems to notice* ESRA *for first time. He sits in middle of his clutter, speaks as if giving fatherly advice.*

GIDEON: Knowing what's important, that's the hard part.
ESRA: Right.
GIDEON (*picks up cassette tape*): The band's called Wire—this is their
    first album. (*Contrite*) Here, you can have it.
ESRA: That's okay.

ESRA *turns away, picks up a cowboy hat, puts it on. Strums guitar.* GIDEON *stands, moves to* ALICE*'s chair, picks up donut box.*

GIDEON (*awkwardly*): Have you had breakfast? Do you want a
    donut?

ESRA *strums an aggressive chord while staring at* GIDEON. GIDEON *tries harder to connect.*

GIDEON: School still closed?

ESRA (*mockingly*): Do you want a donut? (*Strums guitar.*)

GIDEON: Did they give out homework at least?

ESRA: They?

GIDEON (*looks in donut box*): They always give out homework. (*Takes out a donut.*) Here, take the last one.

ESRA: They're Alice's.

IVAN *walks up, a cigar box under his arm, an unlit cigar in his mouth.* GIDEON *slips donut into his jacket pocket; replaces empty box of donuts on* ALICE*'s chair; goes back to sorting his stuff, occasionally bending to adjust something.* ESRA *puts down guitar, picks up video camera, fiddles with it as* IVAN *speaks.*

IVAN (*to* GIDEON): Hey-hey, here he is, my man.

GIDEON *grimaces, nods awkwardly.* IVAN *offers fist.* GIDEON *tentatively returns offer. Fist bump.* ESRA *rolls eyes.*

IVAN (*to* GIDEON): Get this: yesterday, finally, I make it to work—
    walked the whole way—taped to the front door there's this little
    sign—CLOSED. A little red and white sign, like you pick up at a
    hardware store. Like this fifty-story building is a fucken deli.
    CLOSED. That's it.

GIDEON (*disinterested nod*): Huh.

IVAN (*shrugs it off*): Better than having to come up with some bullshit
    alibi. (*Notices* GIDEON*'s stuff.*) What's this—yard sale?

GIDEON (*philosophically*): Organizing. Keeping an eye on my property.

IVAN (*considers this, snorts*): This doesn't look good.

GIDEON: I've been meaning to for a long time.

IVAN: What about the locksmith?

GIDEON: Locksmith? (*Beat.*) I tried all day yesterday. (*Beat.*) They say it could take another day before we're back on the grid. I'll just wait it out.

IVAN *picks up box of donuts, sees it's empty, reads note, tosses it to one side, sits in* ALICE's *chair.*

IVAN (*philosophically*): Food isn't the problem. Plenty of food to go around. Thing is, I don't trust it. A tuna sandwich, left in the sun, two hours—it turns. (*Nods sagely.*) The mayonnaise.

In following exchange ESRA *gets the video camera working, and as she does, the television flickers on, at first showing what she's recording.* ESRA *looks at television, surprised, and experiments with camera, aiming it at sky, at buildings, at* GIDEON's *stuff, at her own face.* IVAN *and* GIDEON *don't notice television.* ESRA *circles them from a few feet away, videotaping. As* IVAN *speaks, the image on the television (and/or a projection on a scrim) becomes a version of his story, as well as some of the stories that follow in this scene.*

While IVAN *speaks,* GIDEON *continues sorting, trying to ignore him.*

IVAN (*cigar box in lap*): I knew this little guy in Africa, lived on a cracker a day. A month straight, one cracker. It's a gene, the "thrifty gene"—Africans got it, we don't, simple as that. Not a calorie is wasted. (*Pats belly.*) I learned something about myself over there—I can go for days without food. (*Musing, then leans into* GIDEON.) You want to know the secret? What to do if you get hungry, I mean really hungry? Empty your mind of all but one thing. Like a meditation, a trance. The zone. Focus your mind—not on a negative thing, on a positive thing. You can train yourself. (*Glances over his shoulder.*) For me, I focus on the women I've been fortunate enough to have . . . been with. (*Opens cigar box, stares into it, closes cigar box.*) I can go for days without eating. (*Taps cigar box.*) Money in the bank.

ESRA (*briefly takes camera down from eye*): I passed a pile of fish rotting on the sidewalk on the way to school. The city's really starting to stink.

IVAN (*ignores her, snaps fingers to get* GIDEON'*s attention*): Gideon, listen—you've got to train your mind. Here's what you do—go anywhere, a bar, the gym, the line at the registry of motor vehicles, anywhere—scope out the best-looking woman in the room, there's always one—what's that joke about lowering your standards?— then, slowly, slowly, move toward her, as if you have all the time in the world. Maybe it takes an hour, maybe two, maybe you don't even make it before she finishes her business and moves on—but it's enough to just keep inching toward her. (*Beat.*) Focus. Visualize. It's a spiritual practice.

ESRA (*briefly takes camera down from eye*): That's what you do when you're hungry?

IVAN (*looks blankly at* ESRA, *then notices her, as if for the first time, smiles*): Hello.

GIDEON *notices* IVAN*'s attention toward* ESRA, *glares at him.* IVAN *turns back to* GIDEON. GIDEON *pays closer attention to* IVAN.

IVAN (*softly*): Once, I'm in line at the bank, behind this knockout. I figure, what the hell, I've got time to kill. So I move in, half a step closer, I'm right up behind her, focused on my breathing—in, out— but after a few minutes I can't stop staring at her neck, *her effen neck*—as if the button was stuck. I keep imagining kissing it, no, I'm wandering across it barefoot, my own private beach. At some point I know she knows, I have to think of something to say, you can say almost anything, the words just start flowing, like turning on a faucet. So we're chatting, in a few minutes we're outside, walking, apparently in the same direction, neither of us in a hurry, and it goes on like that for days, it's summer, we take the train to Coney Island—next thing I know we're on the train every day, we got our own spot.

IVAN *opens cigar box, looks inside, closes cigar box.*

GIDEON (*trying to change subject*): Look . . .
IVAN (*almost bewildered*): I can't say exactly when it turned—one minute I'm on my back, oiled up, the sand, the sun, my arm cradling that beautiful neck, and the same minute I'm trying to remember where the fuck I am, how I got here, who it is beside me—the sun's making my eyelids glow, but all I can come up with, all I can *visualize*, is this dry, barren, poisoned landscape, cracked earth pushing into my back, I'm laid flat out on the salt flats again, nothing growing, no water—at this point we're

engaged, she's pregnant, for chrissakes—and la la la I'm back in this nightmare I've been having off and on since I was a kid, paralyzed, no idea where to go, the world a wasteland and I can't breathe—

IVAN *looks at* ESRA. GIDEON *places himself between them.*

GIDEON: Ivan . . .

IVAN (*still spacy, reaches hand vaguely in* ESRA's *direction*): Off in the distance, way off, a pinpoint of light, faint, nearly imperceptible, I'm not even sure I see it, like in a theater when the lights start going down just before the curtains open and for a split second you think you might be going blind, but it's still there, yes, definitely, that pinpoint of light, and I start to move toward it—which, of course, is away from her. This pinpoint of light, it's a type of oxygen, emanating, somehow, from underground, and even if I walk day and night it'll take the rest of my life to get there, and once I'm there I know it's not going to last—see, I've been there before—you stand over the light, it enters you, but only for a few seconds, and then it fades, and you're left—a mouthful of oxygen, a dry breeze, nothing to do but scan the horizon for the next pinpoint of light.

IVAN *closes eyes, places hands on cigar box.* ESRA *puts down the camera.* GIDEON *glances at* ESRA, *keeping an eye on* IVAN.

IVAN: The darkness around us is deep.
ESRA: What happened to the woman?

IVAN (*looks up, spacy*): Who?

ESRA: The one with the neck.

IVAN *looks down at cigar box, smiles.*

ESRA: You put her in the box?

IVAN (*coming to*): Everything's tiny these days. (*Snaps out of it.*) You gotta travel light.

GIDEON (*to* ESRA): Maybe we should go look for Alice.

ESRA (*ignores him*): Mr. Speck says that humans can live for twenty-one days without water, forty days without food, but only four minutes without oxygen.

IVAN: Speck? What kind of name is Speck?

ESRA (*suddenly excited*): This artist—Chinese, no, Japanese—he spent a year outside, he just never went inside. That was his whole project, his *art*. Mr. Speck showed us the pictures—this Japanese guy walking down a sidewalk, then he's standing in a doorway, then he's lying on the grass. Then there's snow all around him. There was even a picture of him shitting in the river! But think about it, where else would you go? The thing is, by the end of his year outside, he began to blend in, he became almost invisible, like part of the sidewalk, or a bench, until the last photo was just a box in a doorway, a little bigger than a shoe box, and we were supposed to believe he'd somehow bent himself to fit inside it. (*Concerned*) No one knows the side effects of living outside.

IVAN *and* GIDEON *look at* ESRA.

IVAN: Speck. You get older, you realize your teachers were just human—often less than human.

GIDEON (*annoyed*): *I'm* a teacher. (*To* ESRA) I *used* to teach—Harlem, Crown Heights, South Bronx—every day a different school. An arts program. I got them to write poetry. (*To* IVAN) It was a consultant-type thing.

IVAN: Ah, "a consultant-type thing." Nice.

GIDEON (*ignores him; to* ESRA): By the way, humans can live for seventy or eighty days outside with no side effects. After that, no one knows.

ESRA considers this, goes to television, looks at it. Turns to bells, rings several.

IVAN: That won't work. They need power.

Intercom lights up.

INTERCOM: (*Unintelligible static.*)

IVAN, GIDEON stare at intercom. ESRA looks up at building.

Blackout.

SCENE 2

Lights up. Television off. GIDEON *dozing in* ALICE'*s chair, alone, his stuff neatly arranged around him. He wakes, opens his eyes, speaks to audience.*

GIDEON (*rubs face, stretches*): I was in my bedroom, only it wasn't exactly my bedroom. There was a fireplace, but the fireplace in my apartment is plastered over, and this one I could walk right into, I could stand inside it. It was night, I was alone. I took a shit right in the middle of the fireplace. (*Getting it, laughs.*) A pun—where the log should be, I left a log. I found a button I could press and the fireplace would flush. I'd left two turds, but only one washed away. As I was staring at the other one, the remaining one, I heard someone come in behind me, a Czech woman I'd met years ago, Martina, very blond, perhaps the blondest person I've ever seen. The room was dimly lit, but I was embarrassed she'd see my shit. I tried to stand between her and the fireplace, but at that moment two mice scurried across the hearth, and their movements drew our eyes toward them, toward the shit. One of the mice, I realized, was a rat, which filled me with shame as well as fear. I have a primal fear of rats—my mother described every house we lived in as a rathole, I think I might have been bitten by one in my crib. (*Shudders.*) Martina saw the rat too, and now there was no way, I thought, that she'd fuck me, not in that room. But I found another button, which closed off the fireplace, and a plate of poison pellets, which I slid under the closing door. I explained to Martina, telepathically I guess 'cause neither of us spoke, that the rat would eat the pellets, which would make it thirsty, and it would crawl out the chimney to get water, and the water would react somehow with the poison, and it would explode. (*Stares at audience.*)

GIDEON *stands, goes to intercom, rings his bell. Waits. Nothing. Rings his bell again.*

GIDEON (*to audience*): Sometimes I think I've been sleepwalking this whole time. Sometimes I think I'm just waking up. I used to think, What if I lost my key, what then? Well, here we are—this is what then.

GIDEON *presses his bell, stands with his finger on the bell. Slowly turns back to face audience as he speaks.*

GIDEON: I bought a house a few years ago, a ruin. Upstate. When I bought it, everyone told me it would change my life, that it'd give me a sense of rootedness, of belonging. You will own a piece of the goddamn earth, they said. It'll be profound, they said. So I bought the house, and you know what? I felt nothing—no more grounded, no more rooted, no change. I took her there when we first met, we'd go up, spend the weekend—I'd work on it some, and I'd be able to see that it looked better—the paint, the scraping, the trees— I could step back from it all, see it shine, but as soon as I turned away it was as if it never existed. (*Beat.*) It was never real to me, it took up no space inside.

GIDEON *turns back to intercom, presses his bell, leans head against door.*

GIDEON (*into intercom*): I've been thinking—you know what I was afraid of? Suppose we had a kid, suppose the kid came and, like the house, I had no connection to it. Everyone says a kid will change your life, but what if it doesn't? Suppose I can't take it in, suppose I can't tell that it's mine, suppose it isn't real? (*Pause.*) In a few years the house looked just as bad as the first day I walked through the door. One night at dinner I saw a seed roll between the floorboards—I can't stop thinking that it's sprouting into something right now, a little plant, a vine, a vine that will grow into a tree, a tree that will push up through the ceiling, up through the roof, lift the whole thing up to the clouds.

GIDEON *takes finger from bell, turns back to audience.*

GIDEON: In my father's house there are many mansions—I always liked that. Like a riddle, a puzzle. In my father's house there are many mansions. You or me, we couldn't build a house like that, open a door and inside the living room is a mansion, a mansion bigger than the house you just stepped into, a mansion bigger than a mansion. Maybe God gets to cram all his mansions into one house so no one else can live in them, maybe he lets all his angels live there so they don't just wander the clouds looking down on us. Maybe they don't look out for us after all, maybe they're all lost in that mansion, wandering the halls, looking for the bathroom. In my father's house there are many mansions, in my father's bathroom there are many toilets, in my father's kitchen there are many knives, in my father's bedroom there are many pillows.

GIDEON *turns back to door, presses his bell.*

GIDEON (*into intercom, halfheartedly singing*): Get into the groove, boy you've got to prove . . . —it's a nightmare—Madonna takes up more space in my mind than you do.

GIDEON *turns back to audience.*

GIDEON: You wake up one day and you're in your life, you're in your body, and you don't recognize any of it. A meat puppet dangling below your eyes, that's you, that's all you have, a body you don't recognize and a stupid little song rattling in your head. A thought you can't decipher. (*Looks around.*) When did I make this choice, this particular choice? One day folded into the next. (*Halfheartedly singing*) Holiday, it would be so nice . . . —there were years when I thought I'd never get Madonna out of my head, but since I've been outside I haven't thought about her for days. (*Smiles.*)

Blackout.

SCENE 3

Lights up. Television off. IVAN *and* ESRA *are sitting in* ALICE'*s chair.* ESRA *is wearing cowboy hat.* IVAN *is showing* ESRA *photographs from*

his cigar box. GIDEON's *stuff is still spread out neatly around them.*
GIDEON *is nowhere to be seen.*

IVAN (*musing*): Here's one, looks a little like you. Kentucky—skinny as
an otter. Not as young as you, of course—legal, but young. She
asked if I'd gone to Woodstock—Woodstock! I wasn't even born,
but to her I might as well have been a hundred.

ESRA (*judging*): Her eyes are funny.

IVAN: A poet. I've been blessed.

ESRA (*pause*): Do you live outside?

IVAN: Outside? Outside? Darling, do I look like I live outside?

ESRA: Well . . .

IVAN: I'm just waiting for the power to kick back in, like everyone else.
(*Kicks at* GIDEON's *stuff.*) This little adventure, enjoy it while you
can—we'll be back on the grid soon enough.

ESRA (*beat*): Do you have any children?

IVAN: Children?

ESRA: You said the one with the neck was pregnant.

IVAN (*shuts cigar box, looks away for several beats*): I met a kid last
night, not much older than you. Albanian—like a Gypsy only he
said he wasn't a Gypsy. He has this tape of the revolution, a
cassette tape, where the dictator was beheaded or shot or
something, and he has this little Walkman and he puts the
headphones on me and I listen for a while—chaos—people
running, bursts of gunfire, glass breaking, screams. He wants to
know if I can help him sell this little nothing tape to CNN, like it's
breaking news. It happened a few years ago, I guess—I never even
heard of it.

ESRA: So you don't have any children?

IVAN (*laughs*): It's a big world. Nothing would surprise me anymore.

ESRA (*considers this, stands, picks up a toy from* GIDEON'*s stuff*): Mr. Speck says in a few years the world will be filled with computer fog.

IVAN (*snorts*): Speck.

ESRA (*looks up at sky, pretends toy is flying through the air*): Computers will be so small you won't even be able to see them. They'll float around your head, and whatever you want they will make it for you. Like if you want a chair, they will make a chair. Or if you want a sandwich (ESRA *puts down toy, picks up a small folded pile of* GIDEON'*s shirts and holds them up, as if they were a sandwich*)— boom, a sandwich.

IVAN (*nods in grudging agreement*): Tiny's the future. (*Picks up a Polaroid camera from* GIDEON'*s stuff.*) Hey, let me get a picture of you.

ESRA *puts down shirts and picks up a coil of rope, sits in chair. As she speaks, she absentmindedly coils and uncoils rope.* IVAN *fiddles with camera as she speaks.*

ESRA: If I was going to live outside for a year, I'd have a gun—a rifle— what good's a little gun, hidden in your backpack? I watch TV— Oops, sorry, bloodstain on the sidewalk, too late.

IVAN: Your mom'll be back soon, once the power kicks in. Must just be stranded somewhere. I hear they're working on the transformers.

ESRA (*ignores this, coils and uncoils rope*): That artist, the Japanese one? Another time he spent an entire year connected by a big rope to a stranger, a woman he found through the Internet. I mean a newspaper ad, the Internet wasn't even invented. They didn't even know each other. (ESRA *stands, ties rope around her waist.*) They tied the rope around each of their waists and that was it, for one year they didn't untie themselves. Just to see what would happen. I think there was eight feet between them (*measures out eight feet of rope*), so they wouldn't necessarily have to even speak, though of course they did. (*Beat.*) Sounds perfect. (*Pause.*) I'm always losing people.

ESRA *holds up free end of rope to* IVAN. IVAN *takes Polaroid of her. As Polaroid flashes,* ESRA's *Polaroid face appears on television and/or scrim.*

Blackout.

SCENE 4

Sounds of urban chaos from Gypsy's tape. Lights up. Television off. IVAN *is in chair, wearing headphones, Walkman in hand. The rope is now tied around his waist, the other end leading to* ESRA, *who is sleeping behind chair, out of sight. A new flat-screen television is in a box beside him.* GIDEON *is putting all his stuff in trash bags and boxes.*

IVAN (*speaking as lights come up, mimicking tape*): Eeeee, bang bang, ahhhhh—are you shitting me? (*Takes off headphones; then to*

GIDEON) The Gypsy was right where I left him the day before, standing on the side of the road, waiting for a bus that ain't never gonna come. He's not a bad kid, but he's totally fucked. I feel sorry for him, so I walk him to a Best Buy, push him in, in front of us—pandemonium—I say, Here it is, your American dream, and we each walk out with a flat-screen TV. (*Glances over shoulder, speaks softly.*) Thing is, he actually looked kind of sad, like he'd carried this little nothing Walkman all the way from Albania, probably killed someone for it, and now it was worthless.

GIDEON: What are you going to do with a television? There's no power.

IVAN: Gideon, visualize *something*, for chrissakes. I know the old love life ain't going so well, but still . . .

GIDEON (*irritated*): I lost my key.

IVAN: Whatever. (*Turning Walkman over in hands*) I gave him ten bucks for his little tape.

GIDEON (*decisively*): I'm moving everything into storage—today. I rented a unit. Then I'm going to look up a friend who said he'd set me up with a little consulting work. (*Beat.*) To see me through the next few weeks. We used to work together.

IVAN: Ah, yes, "the consultant." Whatever happened to "the locksmith"?

GIDEON (*angry*): I live here. Why are you still here?

IVAN: You got a better place to wait it out?

GIDEON: Wait what out? What, did you lose your key too? I mean, why don't you just go home?

IVAN: I'm just trying to be of help. (*Cleans a spot off his shoe.*)

GIDEON (*incredulous*): You? What? If you wanted to help you'd have brought back some food, not some useless flat-screen.

IVAN: Easy, easy. (*Looks Gideon up and down, stands.*) Listen, Gideon, I've been meaning to tell you—you don't look, how do I say this, put together. The shoes. Here's what you do—next time you're on the subway, check out the other people's shoes. When you see a pair that looks right, that might work for you, make a mental note, then later make it a point to find them. But remember: you can't ask the guy with the nice shoes where he got them, that's the rule. You gotta find them on your own. (*Pause.*) So what's the story— she still up there? (*Gestures up to building.*) What does she do, step over you on her way to work every morning?

GIDEON *turns to bells, rings them all.*

IVAN: The. Power. Is. Out. Gideon, listen—you know what a bottle of Coke will get you in Africa? Buy a girl, any girl, a Coke, and she's yours for the night. Shows you respect her.

GIDEON *rings bells more urgently.*

IVAN: I was in this massage parlor–type place, getting a rubdown, and this little one points to her mouth. She didn't speak a word of English. (*Chuckles.*) I couldn't tell if she was hungry or offering to blow me.

GIDEON *leans head against door.* ESRA *rises from behind chair, yawning, still tied to* IVAN.

IVAN (*glances at* ESRA, *lowers voice*): Gideon—the shoes. Remember what I told you.

GIDEON (*sees* ESRA *tied to* IVAN): What the hell are you doing? (*Moves to untie them.*)

IVAN: Whoa, whoa, whoa—wasn't my idea. She loses people.

ESRA (*to* IVAN): I'm hungry. Is there any food?

IVAN (*to* ESRA): Food, darling, is not a problem—what are you hungry for?

ESRA (*thinks*): Macaroni and cheese.

IVAN: Mac and cheese, right this way.

IVAN *turns to* GIDEON *and shrugs—What can I do?* IVAN *and* ESRA *wander off.* GIDEON *watches them leave.* ALICE *enters behind him, pushing a wheelbarrow full of donuts. She dumps donuts onto her chair, they spill onto sidewalk.*

ALICE: It's a dream, the whole city, wide-open. It's all shadow.

GIDEON: Where've you been? (*Looks to where* IVAN *and* ESRA *exited.*) The girl, have you seen her mother? Where the hell is her mother? She's tied to that guy, that creep. They just wandered off.

ALICE: I know.

GIDEON: You know? (*Sits on his trash bags, worn out.*)

ALICE: She can handle him.

GIDEON: Oh, really? (*Picks up a donut, snorts.*) Donuts.

ALICE: Full of zinc. Makes you dream.

GIDEON: Great.

ALICE: They last forever. They're not for today. (*Begins stacking a few donuts into a small tower on arm of chair.*)

GIDEON (*stands*): I'm leaving, moving my stuff into storage—now. (*Places a donut onto the tower.*) I'm glad you're back.

ALICE: I never left. I was watching you the whole time.

GIDEON (*considers this*): I was at the storage unit this morning. This guy was there, he had a toothbrush—all he had was a toothbrush—it was in a cup on a dolly, the dolly was big enough to move a piano and all he had on it was this little cup. His toothbrush. (*Beat.*) I think people live there. (*Confused*) But they lock you in at night . . .

Intercom lights up, makes static sound.

INTERCOM: Alice.

GIDEON (*looks between intercom and* ALICE): What?

INTERCOM: It's time.

GIDEON (*to* ALICE): Time?

INTERCOM: Alice.

GIDEON *looks at intercom, looks at* ALICE. ALICE *goes to door.*

ALICE (*looks back at* GIDEON): Don't worry—it'll all work out.

ALICE *pulls door open, steps inside. Door closes.* GIDEON *stands, goes to door, tries it, but it's locked. His finger hovers over bells but doesn't ring any.*

Blackout—intercom remains lit for a moment, then goes dark.

ACT THREE
SCENE 1

Stage dark, television flickers on to reveal ALICE's *face, eyes downcast.*
Lights up. GIDEON *is doing push-ups. His stuff is gone; one wheelie*
suitcase remains. IVAN *faces audience, his back to others, attempting to*
juggle three donuts, two cases of beer stacked beside him. ESRA, *still tied*
to IVAN, *stands behind him. She murmurs a little song; swings the rope*
like a jump rope, though no one is jumping. Occasionally ALICE
interjects herself into the conversation, like an echo or a pre-echo, only
half heard by IVAN *and* ESRA. GIDEON *appears to hear* ALICE, *at times*
even repeats what she says, but attempts to ignore her, as if she were a
mosquito in his ear.

IVAN (*to* GIDEON): Anything, the whole city—you pick donuts.

GIDEON (*stops push-ups*): Full of zinc. Makes you dream.

ALICE: Makes you dream.

IVAN: Why not caviar, why not artichokes? (*Snorts.*) I love a good
    donut, but . . .

ESRA: I'm sick of donuts. Mr. Speck says they're poisonous.

ALICE: Depends what kind.

GIDEON: Depends what kind.

IVAN (*mockingly*): Depends what kind. (*Stops juggling, sudden urgency.*) I got it. Listen: what does everyone need? (*Looks around.*) Anyone? No? At night, the sun goes down, what do you look for? Anyone? Come on . . .

ALICE (*mockingly*): A box?

IVAN: A box! And not just any box—a nice big appliance box. Stove, flat-screen—a refrigerator box is best—it's long, you can stretch out—but even dishwasher will do. Here's the money shot . . .

ALICE: Ah, the money shot.

IVAN: After a long day you come home, but something's happened to your box—it's worn out, dirty, waterlogged, a rat's gnawed his way in . . .

ALICE: . . . a dog's pissed on it . . .

IVAN: . . . a dog's pissed on it, a car ran it over, kids came along and clubbed it, used it as a skateboard ramp, your Sterno set it on fire, someone tossed it into a garbage truck . . .

ALICE: . . . the cops declared it illegal . . .

IVAN: . . . the health department condemned it, someone mistook it for a toilet, your friend with scabies infested it, bedbugs moved in, an Indian moved in, a Negro moved in, a crackhead moved in . . .

ALICE: . . . an Indian Negro crackhead . . .

IVAN: . . . a stranger your father your mother your sister, they all moved in, it's crowded, you have no privacy, the glue is giving way . . .

ALICE: . . . sunlight pouring in . . .

IVAN: . . . sunlight is pouring in, you stuck a finger clear through the wall in a rainstorm, the eyeholes are stuffed with tissue—whatever. (*Beat.*) I replace the box. You have a contract with me, I have a contract with you. (*Pause.*) I'm just riffing.

GIDEON *and* ALICE *both laugh, but don't look at each other.* IVAN *seems to hear echo.* GIDEON *resumes push-ups.*

IVAN (*to* ESRA): What? (*To* GIDEON) Enough already with the push-ups. I feel like I'm in prison.

GIDEON (*stops mid-push-up*): These aren't for today. They're for the future.

ESRA (*trying to figure it out, tentatively*): Maybe *this* is prison. Or maybe it's the opposite of prison—instead of never getting out, we just never get in. (*To* IVAN) Hey, is that real, what you said, about Africa? Can we really pay one hundred guys one dollar a day each, and another guy two dollars a day, and the two-dollar guy will make the one-dollar guys do whatever we say? Like if I point my finger, they'll all run in that direction? Or if I say shoot, they'll shoot until I say stop?

IVAN: Our own effen army. (*Sits on cases of beer.*)

ALICE: A fucken army.

GIDEON (*glances at television*): Don't curse.

ESRA (*glances at television, then at* GIDEON): What?

IVAN: God's honest truth.

ESRA (*excitedly*): I think we should all go to Africa.

IVAN: I'm ready anytime. Full of potential, that place.

GIDEON (*to* IVAN): What's wrong with you?

ESRA: I've got like three thousand dollars in my college fund. That means we could hire (*adds in head*) twenty guys for a year.

IVAN (*adds in head*): Ten or twelve, realistically.

ESRA: Is that enough for an army? How much do you have?

ALICE: This should be good.

GIDEON: Africa? You can't even get downtown.

IVAN (*takes out a beer*): Obstacles, my friend, are an illusion—you believe obstacles to be real. That's your problem.

GIDEON: Are you going to untie your little friend before you go? Or is she just an illusion?

IVAN: It's her idea.

ESRA: I don't see what's wrong with being tied to someone. Better than being married.

ALICE: Depends on who you're tied to.

GIDEON: Depends on who you're tied to.

IVAN (*opens beer, takes sip*): They have this gin over there, made from bananas. Bungo juice.

IVAN *offers his bottle to* GIDEON, *who refuses.* IVAN *offers bottle to* ESRA, *who takes it, takes a sip, makes face, passes it back.*

ALICE: Bungo juice.

IVAN: I had a friend—not a friend, really, a guy I knew—we'd drink bungo juice on his porch at sunset, looking out over the veldt. He kept those people on his land, the tall herdsmen, what do you call them? Maori? No. Mandingo? Manatee? Something. The tall ones. He had a mansion—believe me, it doesn't take much, over there—down below he had all these guys, the tall ones, living in huts, just like they would out in the bush. (*Beat.*) Except there was a fence so they wouldn't just wander off. He enjoyed looking at them, the way they moved. (*Musing*) Surprisingly elegant, those people.

ALICE: Surprising they didn't cut your head off.

GIDEON (*mutters*): Surprising they didn't cut your head off.

ESRA (*excitedly*): Let's all go. Africa.

GIDEON: What about your mother? She'll be back any minute.

ESRA: She can come too.

ALICE *whistles a crooked tune—the theme from* The Good, the Bad and the Ugly. IVAN *and* ESRA *look around, as if they can hear it.* GIDEON *continues with his push-ups.*

Blackout.

SCENE 2

Lights up. GIDEON *is in* ALICE*'s chair, looking through* IVAN*'s photos.* ESRA *enters, pushing wheelbarrow,* IVAN *tipsy inside.* IVAN *and* ESRA *are still tied together.*

IVAN (*holds up one finger*): This finger moves hundreds of thousands of dollars a minute. (*Poking the air*) Boop, boop, boop.

Television flickers on. Africa, Serengeti.

ESRA (*to* IVAN): Look, Africa! You need to get back there. Chant it—Africa, Africa, Africa.

IVAN (*half rises, bleary; squints at television, smiles*): Fucken Africa. Pay someone a dollar to stand beside your car with a stick. (*Lowers himself back into wheelbarrow, self-satisfied.*)

GIDEON (*snorts*): Africa.

ESRA: He knows a lot. He has a plan.

GIDEON: A plan? Look at him—I know why I'm here, I know why you're here. Why's he here? (*Goes up to wheelbarrow;* IVAN *appears to have dozed off.*) I don't believe anything about him. (*Points to television.*) You could get all he knows from the nature channel. (*Goes back to chair, holds up a photo.*) These women, his "girlfriends"—for all we know he could have found them in the trash. (*Finds Polaroid of* ESRA; *is shocked.*) Why's your picture here?

ESRA *takes picture, looks at it, then looks up to tops of buildings.*

ESRA (*conspiratorially*): There's cameras everywhere. (*Puts photo back in box.*) What if, tomorrow, that door opened and this has been a reality show, the whole thing, the whole time?

Television flickers; ALICE's *face appears, replacing Africa.* ALICE *stares straight ahead, calm.* ESRA *looks at television.*

ESRA: Power's back.

ESRA *goes to bells, rings one, stands back, looks up at building, waits.*

ESRA (*pointing up*): At night, a face peeks at me from behind that curtain. That's my room. She thinks I'm asleep, I let her think that. I keep my head in the shadows. Last night I waved a little, just a little wave, to see what she would do. (*Waves up.*)

ALICE *waves.*

GIDEON (*gently*): I never see anyone up there.
ESRA (*turns on him*): Who do you work for?
ALICE (*amused*): Who *do* you work for?
GIDEON (*glances at* ALICE, *confused*): What am I supposed to do?
ESRA (*softer*): I don't understand how I became one of you.
GIDEON: One of what? What am I?
ALICE (*snorts*): That seems kind of obvious.

GIDEON *glares at* ALICE. ESRA *moves wheelbarrow to bells, rings them all. Stands back. Looks up at building. Puts ear against door.*

ESRA: I can almost hear them in there. (*Beat.*) I don't care. It's better
   out here. I don't think I could breathe if I was back inside.
   (*Assumes* IVAN's *voice, as if lecturing, puncturing air with finger.*)
   What we need are assets, not liabilities. Renting an apartment is a
   liability. Your mother, a liability. Own things that generate income.
   Don't live in the apartment, get someone else to pay to live in the
   apartment. Get other people to work *for* you.
ALICE: What do you say to that, Teach?
GIDEON (*to* ALICE): I think it's bullshit.
ESRA: Ivan made a fortune doing it.
ALICE (*to* GIDEON): Go ahead.
GIDEON (*annoyed*): Go ahead what?
ESRA: Are you talking to the TV?
ALICE: Tell her.

INTERCOM: Whoizit?

GIDEON (*moves to untie* ESRA *from* IVAN): Go. Don't come back.

ESRA: Go where?

INTERCOM (*annoyed*): Whoizit?

Blackout.

SCENE 3

The first few chords of "Come Together" play over and over. Lights up. Television off. Stage dimly lit. Donuts stacked in small towers on chair, on sidewalk, most still in a small pile. IVAN, ESRA, *and* GIDEON *stand in shadows, eyes half closed, zombie-like, as if sleepwalking. Their movements are minimal, stylized—keening, prayerful, twitchy. As each is illuminated, his or her eyes open wide. Intercom voice is alternately deadpan, determined, playful, annoyed. Intercom lights up. Music stops. As intercom and then* ALICE *speak, corresponding images are projected onto scrim.*

INTERCOM: Hello, birdy.

IVAN*'s face lit, briefly.* IVAN *smiles.*

INTERCOM: Hello, cruel world.

ESRA*'s face lit, briefly.* ESRA *smiles.*

INTERCOM: I am not now nor have I ever been . . . (*Beat.*) . . . A lock. A key. A cock. A tongue . . . (*Beat.*) . . . A buzzer. A bell. A finger. A gun. (*Beat.*) Ah, here come ol' flattop . . .

GIDEON's *face lit, briefly.* GIDEON *smiles.*

INTERCOM: One and one and one is three . . . (*Beat.*) A lock. A key. A brick. The sea . . .

Television flickers on. ALICE's *face appears on TV and/or on scrim— calm, beatific.* IVAN's, ESRA's, *and* GIDEON's *faces lit. They each twitch.*

ALICE: Knock knock.

Light off IVAN's *and* GIDEON's *faces.* ESRA *smiles.*

ALICE: Now you say, *Who's there?*

ESRA's *smile turns to concern.*

ALICE: Let's try that again—Knock knock.

ESRA's *eyes look around, panicked.*

ALICE (*gently*): You can do it—*Who's there?*

ESRA *closes eyes, as if trying not to hear. Twitches.*

ALICE: Knock knock. (*Mimicking* ESRA) Who's there? (*Regular voice*) Occupying army.

ESRA *rolls head, as if keening.*

ALICE (*mimicking* ESRA): Occupying army who? (*Regular voice*) Just kidding—we don't knock.

ESRA *stops keening, looks straight ahead. Light off* ESRA*'s face.*

INTERCOM: Monkey finger. Coca-Cola. Ol' flattop. Holy Roller.

IVAN*'s face is illuminated, his eyes open.*

ALICE: This guy was fucking a fat chick—she was so fat that he ended up falling right into her cunt.

IVAN *seems to remember something from his past; concerned.*

ALICE: He wandered around inside her for a while, lost, until he saw a light in the distance, and so he went toward it . . .

IVAN*'s face twitches.*

ALICE: . . . It was another man, carrying a flashlight. I lost my car keys, the other man says. If you help me find them we can drive out of here.

IVAN*'s eyes close. Light off* IVAN*'s face.*

INTERCOM: One and one and one is three. One thing I can tell you is . . .

IVAN*'s,* ESRA*'s, and* GIDEON*'s faces illuminated. Each is wide-eyed.*

ALICE: When I said I wanted to be a comedian, they all laughed.

IVAN, ESRA, *and* GIDEON *smile.*

ALICE: They're not laughing now.

IVAN, ESRA, *and* GIDEON *consider this.*

ALICE (*generously*): I was always right in front of you.
　　(*Wearily*): One and one and one is three.

IVAN, ESRA, *and* GIDEON *close eyes, keen slightly.*

ALICE (*resignedly*): Well, well, well, we're all here.
　　(*Seriously*): Did you think it would last forever?
　　(*Beat.*) How can I help?
　　(*Beat.*) Donut? Bungo juice? Bus fare home?
　　(*Beat.*) Hello, cruel world.
　　(*Beat.*) The good times are killing us.
　　(*Beat.*) I am not now nor have I ever been . . .
　　(*Beat.*) . . . unhappy for you.

IVAN, ESRA, *and* GIDEON *stop swaying. Their faces return to shadow.* ALICE *closes eyes, television goes dark. Only light is now from intercom.*

INTERCOM: A door. A bell. A brick. A lock. Brick upon brick upon day upon day, count the stairs up, a number nailed to a door. A lock, a cunt, a cock, a key, a window the color of air. Sit in your chair, stare at your wall, water hidden in pipes, electricity buried in wires. Stare at your wall, the paint has a name, one day for no reason it's gone. What will you do? Will you stand from your chair, will you put your hand out, walk right through the wall like a dream? There's always a room filled with people you don't know, a room that was always never there. You're outside a door; the number is yours; the key, it fell from your hand. You once had a mother, you once slept inside her, and then you slept beside her. Your mother, once she had you, you slowly outgrew her, no way to fit back inside. You once had a lover, you once slept inside her, one day you simply got lost. A finger a knee, a cock a key, a throat a bell, a lock a cunt—one and one and one is three.

Blackout.

SCENE 4

Lights up. IVAN *is standing beside wheelbarrow, bleary, rope still tied to his waist.* GIDEON *is in* ALICE's *chair.* GIDEON *pushing his feet into a large trash bag and pulling it up the length of his body, duct-taping it around his ankles, his waist, his chest. Beside him, a camp stove is*

*heating a pan of water, donuts stacked in a few small towers beside it.
The television flickers on—*ALICE*'s head appears on screen.* GIDEON
glances at television while ALICE *speaks, but tries to ignore her. At first*
IVAN *apparently doesn't hear or notice* ALICE.

ALICE (*staring straight ahead*): Grasping at straws. (*Beat.*) When do
    you ever actually get to see a man drowning? Maybe once in your
    life, maybe twice, if you're lucky. At that moment you either save
    him or you don't. You either try or you don't . . .

IVAN *turns toward sound of television, moves toward it, accidentally
kicks over a tower of donuts.*

GIDEON (*annoyed*): Careful.
IVAN (*confused*): They changed the channel.
ALICE: . . . and then you go on, you live with it, your choice. Maybe
    you froze when you could have jumped, maybe from that moment
    on you tell yourself that nothing could have been done. Maybe
    that's what you have to tell yourself, maybe it's true. Maybe your
    name was in the paper as a hero, maybe as an onlooker, maybe the
    person drowning was you.
IVAN (*still looking at television*): Gideon, I heard about some low-
    income housing about to open up. To buy in, all you have to be is a
    minority. Ten thousand down, a few months later we flip it, we
    each walk away, fifty thousand in our pockets. (*Beat.*) We just need
    to scrape together the down payment.
ALICE: Ah, the down payment.
IVAN (*points to television*): Did you hear that?

GIDEON: I'm not a minority.

IVAN (*still looking suspiciously at television*): I have some Dominican blood. On my mother's side. You can be the silent partner.

ALICE (*looks down at* GIDEON): Have you ever noticed the sign in the pet shop window across the street? FREE BIRD WITH EVERY CAGE. I used to stare at that sign for hours. Yesterday I went inside, and all the birds were gone—all that was left was cages.

IVAN: Hey, it's as if she's talking to you.

ALICE (*looks hard at* IVAN): You know what you need?

IVAN*'s eyes widen.*

ALICE: A sign—*BUS FARE HOME, FREE BIRD WITH EVERY CAGE, ETERNAL DAMNATION—ASK ME HOW.* It'll make you invisible. That's what signs are for.

GIDEON *and* ALICE *laugh.* IVAN *looks back and forth between them.* GIDEON *goes back to his taping.*

IVAN (*to* GIDEON, *tentatively*): The deadline for applying is the end of today. (*Beat.*) Gideon—you in or out?

GIDEON: Out. But you should do it—really.

ALICE: Really.

IVAN (*warily*): I've got to get downtown.

ALICE (*mockingly*): Downtown.

IVAN: Busy day.

ALICE: Busy busy.

IVAN, *shaken, leaves, glancing back at television.*

ALICE (*to* IVAN*'s retreating back*): If that's where you want to spend
   eternity. (*Looks straight ahead.*) Invisible's easy—you don't have to
   announce a thing—stop picking up your mail, let the milk go
   rancid on your counter, order Chinese and don't answer the bell.
   Say you'll be somewhere at ten and never show. Leave your cell
   phone on the edge of a bridge, then call yourself and hang up.
   Invisible is a window left open—just step through it. Everyone will
   assume you simply vaporized. Some will look up at the clouds they
   call heaven; some will look down, as if you might still be falling.
   Most will assume you jumped, up or down, over or out, and you
   might as well have—you no longer occupy the same space in the
   world. The little gasps of breath you are allotted—give them to
   someone else. The promise of eternity—who knows? I had a
   husband once, he left because I couldn't promise to meet him in
   eternity. He said, Why are we wasting our time? He wanted a
   promise of eternity but was afraid of wasting time—wrap your
   mind around that one. Eternity, ha—seems unlikely, at this
   juncture, that they're keeping their best hidden.

ESRA *rides up on scooter. She tries the door, rings the bell, looks up at
windows.* ALICE *looks straight ahead, calm.* GIDEON *continues taping
trash bag.*

ESRA (*to* GIDEON): I can't believe my mom's not back. She's so dumb.
   (*Beat—concerned*) What are you doing?

GIDEON (*trying to sound upbeat*): Oh, you know me. Preparing. Could you put your finger here?

GIDEON *gestures to bag, wants* ESRA *to cinch it tight around his waist so he can tape it tightly.* ESRA *kneels, holds bag absentmindedly while she speaks.*

ESRA: You know what Mom calls me? "Ass-bastard." *You little ass-bastard.* (*Laughs.*) You know what I do to her? (*Scratches her cheek slowly with her middle finger, laughs.*) She's so dumb she doesn't even notice. (*Looks up at building, concerned.*) She's supposed to be back by now.

GIDEON (*attempts to sound parental*): So, *sunshine,* tell me, what did you learn in school today?

ESRA: Nothing.

GIDEON (*desperate*): Tell me one thing. Anything.

ESRA: School's closed.

GIDEON (*feigns optimism*): Well, that won't last forever. We just have to get through the next few days. (*Points to television.*) Power's back.

ESRA (*looks at television, sighs*): Africa. I really just wanted to see a monkey. (*Beat.*) You know what I do in my apartment? I see if I can make it around the entire room without touching the floor. (*Acts this out as she speaks.*) I start on the couch (*she jumps onto* ALICE*'s chair*), then jump onto the windowsill (*she moves from chair to window ledge*), then I put one foot on the doorknob and swing over to the mantel (*she jumps onto* GIDEON*'s wheelie suitcase, knocks it over*).

GIDEON: That's a good skill to have.

ESRA: My mom comes in sometimes when I'm on the doorknob and doesn't even see me.

GIDEON: Someone's answering the bells again.

ESRA (*looks at bells, doesn't move toward them*): I'm working on a project for school. I'm going to interview everyone who lives in my building now or anyone I can find who used to live in it.

ESRA *takes video camera out of her backpack.*

ESRA: It's due in a week.

ESRA *turns camera on, looks through viewfinder, aims it at* GIDEON.

ESRA: So . . .

GIDEON (*uncertain*): I don't know.

ESRA: You can say anything. I'll edit it later. I want to get Alice too. (*Looks around for* ALICE.)

ALICE (*to* GIDEON): Go ahead, tell her how you ended up here.

GIDEON (*to* ALICE, *angrily*): I can go back inside anytime.

ESRA: Who are you talking to?

ALICE: Who *are* you talking to?

GIDEON (*to* ESRA): Hmm?

ESRA: Just say, "My name is Gideon, I live here . . ."

GIDEON (*long pause*): My name is Gideon. (*Beat.*) I live here, in this building, right here. Right up there, on the third floor. That's my window, right there. (*Beat.*) I don't know what else to say.

ESRA: Tell about your job.

GIDEON: My job? (*Beat.*) Well, I'm a teacher. A consultant. I ride the
subway to work every day, a different school every day. (*Musing*)
On the train, someone's always asleep next to me—the whole train,
sometimes, is sleeping—all us sleepers, half the time we nearly miss
our stops. (*Beat.*) If I'm going to Far Rockaway, there's this one
spot where the train rises up from underground—below, as far as
you can see, is a graveyard—bleeding crosses, marble teardrops,
life-sized angels—most just open an eye, then fall back asleep, but I
wake up from whatever little dream I'm having in this blast of pure
daylight— (*Excited*) You know what I figured out—that if we didn't
come out of the ground right then we'd be tunneling through
corpses. (*Musing*) All us sleepers. Sometimes I do this thing—I
turn my head and look closely at whoever's sleeping beside me,
sometimes I look right in his ear. Or her ear. Sometimes I even lean
over and whisper "I love you," even though I've never seen this
person before. (*Beat.*) For a while I imagined I could love anyone.
ESRA (*incredulous*): You look into his ear?
ALICE: You can't love everyone. Probably why she threw you out.
GIDEON (*spacy*): I don't miss it, that subway, every morning, not really.

Blackout.

AFTERWORD

One day, a couple years ago, I found myself flying on a bankrupt airline over a flooded city. I was on my way to Texas, an itinerant poet off to teach for a few months. The man next to me was trying to get to the ruined city we were passing over, hoping to return home, or to what was left of his home. The airport hadn't reopened yet, so he was landing in Houston and planning, hoping, to rent a car, follow the highway up the coast. After listening to the story of how he'd escaped the storm, of what might be waiting for him when he returned, I asked him what he thought of the federal response. *They'd done all they could do*, he said—*It was a flood, after all, an act of God.* I asked if he thought they could have gone in sooner, stopped some of the mayhem, the desperation. Leaning into me, he whispered, *If I was black I'd have it made right now. I could ask for anything and it'd be delivered right to my door.*

When asked what his plays were about, Harold Pinter once famously and facetiously replied that they were all about "the weasel under the cocktail cabinet." Pinter insists that he was merely trying "to frustrate this line of inquiry," but his apocryphal response is still bandied about quite seriously, if only because the image suggests a certain menace hiding beneath the seemingly mundane, which could, in fact, describe at least some of Pinter's work. "For me the remark meant precisely nothing," Pinter claims, and there's no reason to doubt him, except for the fact that it could have been uttered by one of his characters and thereby perhaps offers a glimpse into Pinter's subconscious, or at least into the bad neighborhood of his mind. Or maybe it's merely a glimpse into the bad neighborhood of my mind, for now it is me still holding on to this tossed-off image, attempting to weigh it down with significance.

If the racism that man on the plane felt free to utter were an animal, I find myself imagining, it might look like a weasel. The storm, it seemed, had pulled back the curtain on a level of racism that white America generally prefers to pretend doesn't exist—hiding under the cocktail cabinet, as it were. After the storm, there followed a brief moment of hope that now that it was revealed, dragged into the light for all to see, we would, as a nation, rise up and deal with it. But right away some said that what the storm revealed wasn't a weasel at all, that there was nothing under the cocktail cabinet, or at least nothing to concern ourselves with. One local politician even said publicly that nature had in five days done what he'd been trying to accomplish during his entire political life—that is, get the poor people out of New Orleans. In this light, a storm might be viewed as an opportunity. Naomi Klein recently coined a phrase for this phenomenon: "disaster capitalism." She writes: "Not so long ago, disasters were periods of social leveling, rare moments when atomized communities put divisions aside and pulled together. Today they are moments when we are hurled further apart, when we lurch into a radically segregated future where some of us will fall off the map and others ascend to a parallel privatized state, one equipped with well-paved highways and skyways, safe bridges, boutique charter schools, fast-lane airport terminals, and deluxe subways."*

———

*Naomi Klein, "Disaster Capitalism," *Harper's Magazine*, October 2007, p. 50.

Alice Invents a Little Game and Alice Always Wins is, in part, about the aftermath of a disaster, though exactly what that disaster is remains unclear. The play came about, as nearly everything does, by something seemingly insignificant snagging onto someone's (my) consciousness, or unconsciousness. The insignificant something, this time, was a photograph of the aftermath of a blackout in New York City—lights out, trains dead, businessmen stranded overnight, unable to make it back to Westchester, forced to sleep on sidewalks and park benches. What caught my attention was their suits—very high-end. Not that I wore suits, but sometimes, privately, I imagined that one day I'd be the kind of person who could wear a suit.

Initial speculation was that the blackout might be "terrorist related," but the terrorists were quickly written out of the story, leaving room for other theories. Tapes had recently been released of young Enron workers chatting gleefully about their plan to black out California for a few days, thereby instilling a fear that would then justify jacking up the prices. On the tapes, two young guns can be heard joking about "Granny having to drain her pension" to pay her bills. It didn't seem so far-fetched that this moneymaking scheme was being replicated in New York, but it seems that this particular blackout turned out to be merely a symptom of our crumbling infrastructure—a transformer, maybe in Canada, had malfunctioned, shutting off the power to a huge swath of the eastern United States. Simple, old-fashioned negligence and decay, another day at the tail end of the empire.

But those suits—something about the quality of the fabric against the coarseness of a cardboard box lodged itself in my subconscious. I had spent the previous two years shuttling between Rome and Africa—

Tanzania, mostly—and I couldn't help but do the math. Some of these suits cost ten times the yearly pay of most Africans—I have a friend in Tanzania who had lived for a while on a cracker a day. While I was there, the government, in order to comply with World Bank "austerity" rules, was in the process of privatizing basic services. The electric company had recently been sold to a South African firm, and I swear they paid someone to flick the power off and on several times a day, if just to make us appreciate this miracle of light we were being offered.

I moved to Rome in the fall of 2001 in order to finish a book on homelessness and my father. One morning, a few weeks after I arrived, I woke up with the flu. I staggered outside to get some juice and painkillers to tide me over, and when the door slammed shut behind me I realized I'd locked myself out. A sick feeling washed over me as I remembered that the landlord had told me that there was only one key to that door, and it was now sitting on the kitchen table. I had my cell phone, but it was early, and I knew the landlord slept late. I left a message and got some tea, my head pounding. My Italian was rudimentary at best, and within an hour I ended up in the park, sleeping on a bench, my cell phone battery slowly draining its charge, the landlord still not calling back.

If I hadn't been writing about the years my father had spent homeless, those few hours spent outside might not have hit me so hard. Deep inside I had always been afraid of becoming him, but I hadn't expected it to hinge on something as simple, as obvious, as a key. What passed through my mind as I lay on that bench perhaps passed through a few of those businessmen's minds that night they found themselves outside: What if this never ends, what if I simply never make it back inside? Could it really be this simple, could it be this blameless?

Some say that in dreams all the characters are manifestations of our subconscious selves. Sounds about right to me. Unfortunately (or not), since these selves are shadows, we often do not recognize them. Even before Freud, the Greeks recognized this—think of Oedipus and his confusions.

When I was younger, I worked with the homeless for many years, gravitating to the "psych guys," as we called them, though for the first year or so when I wrote about them in the daily log, I misspelled the word "psych" as "psyche." I could sit and talk to them for hours— much of what they said was impossible, but some of it made sense. I knew even then that I was attempting to access something in my own psyche, some part of my own madness. I couldn't know it then, but I was also waiting for my father to arrive, to step back into my life.

This was the mid-1980s. As more and more people began appearing on the streets of American cities and towns, some argued that we were accepting what would have previously been unacceptable, and that it could be argued that as a consequence of accepting the unacceptable, America, all of us, were becoming psychically homeless. At the time I merely wondered why more of us didn't simply run down the streets screaming, like some of the psych guys I knew did.

The title *Alice Invents a Little Game and Alice Always Wins* is another one of those things that got snagged on my (un)consciousness. It is the title of an experimental film that a friend, the filmmaker Hubert

Sauper, told me about but that I have yet to see—*Alice erfindet ein kleines Spiel, das Alice gewinnt* (1989). It was directed by Claudia Messmer, who lives in Vienna. The title rolled around in my head for a while, found some purchase, and kept rising up to the surface. Something in me liked the idea of this woman, this Alice, inventing a game that only she could win. It seemed both powerful and insane. Alice is also the name of my grandmother—Allie—the woman who raised my brother and me, the one who fed us the nights our mother was working late or out on a date. It is likely one of the first names I ever uttered. She was nothing like the Alice in this play, as far as I can tell. In the book I wrote on the homeless, I also used the name as a pseudonym for a woman I knew who lived in a box.

Sometimes, when the phrase "Alice Invents a Little Game and Alice Always Wins" was rolling around in my head, before the writing began, I imagined Alice to be a metaphor for America, and her game like a game of musical chairs, with the idea that the music was about to end. Musical chairs always seemed the prototypical capitalist game, creating a sense of desperation and competition among friends. Who is it that gets to take away one chair each time, and where do the chairs go, and who lifts the needle from the vinyl? That was an idea I had in the initial drafts, but in the end the Alice in the play does not seem like the one who lifts the needle from the vinyl, or the one who takes away the chairs. In these pages, she is as bewildered as everyone else, if slightly more accepting of that bewilderment, which gives her whatever power she may have. She is, perhaps, simply one of the many who found a way to live without a chair, so to speak, earlier than the rest of us.

Sometimes it seems like this great game of musical chairs we've been playing in America is coming to an end, that the music is stopping more and more frequently, that there are fewer and fewer chairs. Not to be apocalyptic, but as I touched on earlier, we did lose a major American city a couple of years ago to a hurricane and then simply left the survivors to fend for themselves. I will admit, though, that it is (perhaps) my temperament to see disasters where others see opportunity—I hear Mardi Gras went well this year. I spent several years working with the homeless, and then several more working in New York City public elementary schools where half the students lived in shelters. I saw homeless people everywhere, invisible to most—I knew they were homeless because I knew them, or I could recognize the signs.

But I am getting away from myself. I merely wanted to say a few words about how this play came into being. *Alice* began as a handful of images, of phrases, which eventually led to the images and phrases gathering some energy around them, until they began to generate their own energy—an image cluster, a closed image system, which can be a beautiful thing but can also be a dangerous thing. Think of the idea of torture, which at this moment in America seems to have a lot of energy swirling around it, largely as a result of the image of a ticking bomb, about to explode, and the madman sitting before you, refusing to reveal the location. This is a very powerful, yet deeply flawed, image system, and it has led to some horrific abuses. It is also a flawed rhetorical argument, based as it is on a hypothetical situation that is unlikely ever to manifest itself in reality—it is unlikely you will have the madman in the chair before you, that you will know he has planted a bomb and yet you will not know its location. An equivalent argument is this: If you knew the baby in the carriage before you was to grow up to become another Hitler, would you be justified in bashing its brains out with a hammer? It seems obvious that there is no way to know who the baby will grow up to be, and even if you believe to your soul it to be true, you would be a madman to act on this belief. As epistemological games, these musings can fill many bong-hit-filled nights, but in the past few years this "ticking bomb" has, unfortunately, been used to justify changing the Constitution and subverting the Geneva Conventions. It has led, once again, to many of us being willing to accept the unacceptable.

Sophocles' play *Philoctetes* begins with Odysseus sailing back to the island he abandoned an injured Philoctetes on years earlier. Philoctetes, it seems, is the keeper of a bow that, it is prophesied, is needed to win the Trojan War. Odysseus sends Neoptolemus ashore to convince Philoctetes, whose gangrenous foot is driving him mad with pain, to hand over this bow for the greater good. The play deals, in part, with rhetoric and the uses and abuses of argument. *Philoctetes* argues that it is all right to manipulate the truth for a greater end: that is, to win, and thereby end, a war. Neoptolemus is not convinced. In the midst of these rhetorical arguments are moments of dark humor:

PHILOCTETES: (*Screams in pain.*)

NEOPTOLEMUS: It isn't the pain of your sickness coming upon you, is it?

PHILOCTETES: Not at all—on the contrary, I feel like I'm rallying, just now— Oh, gods!*

Rallying. These days, the manipulation of the truth feels smaller, often simply for accumulating more wealth, which is why it is said we've become too small for tragedy. Now we read books with titles like *Rich Dad, Poor Dad* and watch television shows like *The Apprentice*, which, it could be argued, are simply handbooks to justify the exploitation of others. In *Alice Invents a Little Game and Alice Always Wins*, Ivan understands this, Gideon resists it, and Esra is caught between the two. Alice, who may or may not have invented this rigged game, vanishes in the end, seemingly into the television, to become as invisible and pervasive as the air we breathe.

—Nick Flynn, 2007

*Sophocles, *Philoctetes*, trans. Carl Phillips (Oxford: Oxford University Press, 2003).